She was tiny but MIGHTY, not the other way around.

A doubt in her mind, it couldn't be found.

TWO PIECES OF ONE

A JOURNEY TO WALKING TOGETHER WITH THE SELF

JESSICA MARY SHULVER

ISBN 979-8-89699-774-0

She knew she was bright and always asked "why?"

She didn't understand why not all of the adults knew, so sometimes she cried.

She needed to understand why the sky was blue, oh and also the sea!

"Why do all of these big questions keep coming to ME?"

Her dreams were very big... And yes, it was noticed.

In fact, people often thought her dreams were HOCUS POCUS!

Still... She believed in magic, she knew it in her heart.

Dancing her way through the day was a perfect place to start.

People stared as she grew, loud and proud and bold.

She began to wonder whether she should believe what she had been told.

Should she give it all up for what the big ones and the movies said?

Should she live a whole different life instead?

She tried... It was fun... But only for a while.

One day she looked in the mirror, it was hard to crack a smile.

Time passed and she grew to be a little grey, too early... Where did her magic go?

There was a time where it was absolutely ALWAYS on show!

She wondered and questioned and looked at herself...

Had she been hiding away behind a really thick shell?

She peeped out and stepped down, just ever so gently... Though this time, she spotted a face in the mirror that looked really friendly.

She was younger and brighter... She shone almost like the sun.

She had met her before... She suddenly felt stunned!

She reached out and smiled with her most gifted left hand... And finally, she felt that she understands.

It was her that she'd stared at, when she gently stepped out...

Of the shell that kept her safe for some time... That actually stopped her from expressing what she was uniquely about.

She was magic and bravery, all mixed in one.

A beam of understanding and smarts and did I mention fun?

She could make things and break things and start all over again.

She decided that day, to be her very best friend.

To this day, they walk together... Always towards the sun.

Because on either side of the shell, were two pieces of one.

The End.